# Keep Her Captivated

## Lead Your Relationship To Its Maximum Potential

By Jordan Gray

Relationship Coach at
www.jordangrayconsulting.com

September 2014
Copyright © 2014 Jordan Gray
All rights reserved worldwide.
ISBN: 1502350238
ISBN-13: 978-1502350237

# Table of Contents

Author's Comments ................................................................ 5

Introduction .............................................................................. 7

Disclaimer ................................................................................ 11

**Part 1 - Effectively Expressing Your Love**  **13**

    Power Compliments ........................................................ 16

    Subtle Gestures ................................................................ 22

    Calibrated Surprises ........................................................ 27

    Piercing Conversations .................................................... 30

**Part 2 - Improving Communication**  **33**

    Being A Great Listener ................................................... 36

Playing On The Same Team ............................................... 45

Respectfully Expressing Your Needs ............................. 49

## Part 3 - Taking the Lead          53

Being a Loving Leader ...................................................... 55

Opening Her Emotionally ................................................ 59

Getting Over Arguments & Apologizing ..................... 64

## Part 4 - Supercharging Your Sex Life    71

Sexual Polarity .................................................................... 73

Power Compliments .......................................................... 78

Pleasuring Her Physically ................................................ 82

Being a Sexual Beast ......................................................... 91

What To Do Now ............................................................. 103

Closing Comments .......................................................... 105

About the Author ............................................................ 107

# Author's Comments

"*After all of these years, I still feel excited knowing that I am coming home to him.*"

My grandmother's words about her relationship with my grandfather could not have been simpler or more eloquent. After being married for 56 years, she still adores him.

What is it that makes certain relationships thrive, even after decades of commitment? What is it about other relationships that allows them to fail?

Over the past five years, I've worked with more than 1,000 clients in every step of the relationship process- from helping single clients get married to revitalizing long-term relationships and improving sex lives. Some of my favorite clients are those that are in good relationships but want to lead these relationships to their maximum potential. These are my favorite people to work with because they are taking a proactive approach to this crucial part of their lives. If you invest time and energy into your relationship, every element of your life will be enriched.

I want men to man up when it comes to their intimate lives. I want to help inspire the kind of loving relationships that other couples look to as role models. I want to encourage men to reignite the passion in their relationships.

My mission is to bring men to their full potential in their intimate lives; a thriving romantic relationship enriches every aspect of both their lives and the lives of their partners.

The goal of this book is to take an actionable, simple, and direct approach to making a relationship thrive. I want to take the guess work out of what makes a relationship amazing.

So through my personal experience, as well as through the compilation of data from over a hundred interviews (with what most people would consider massively successful long-term couples), I feel like I have cracked the code. I've identified what makes the foundation for a spectacular relationship. And, in this book, I aim to present that information in a clear and actionable way.

So buckle up, you're in for a treat.

Dedicated to your success,

Jordan Gray

# Introduction

As modern men, we are constantly learning how to accumulate more wealth, how to get into better shape, and how to become the best versions of ourselves possible. However, rarely do we put the same time and energy into learning how to become better partners.

The absurd thing about this is that your relationship affects all of those things: financial success, physical health and emotional well being. By reading this book, you will develop a healthier relationship with your partner, and I guarantee that you will see improved results in all of other areas of your life.

In the following pages, you will find the tools that will help you better understand your relationship, and as a result, improve its health to the point where it can *thrive.*

A thriving relationship is one where communication flows freely, where both partners feel loved and supported by each other, and where the sex is connected and transformational.

The book is broken down into four main parts: Effectively Expressing Your Life, Improving Communication, Taking The Lead and Supercharging Your Sex Life. In each section, you will find explanations, examples, and exercises that will help you understand what it takes to make your relationship remarkable.

It's helpful to understand a couple core concepts before getting into the thick of it. First of all, what role do you and your personal level of happiness have to do with where your relationship is currently standing?

## Your Relationship's Health Starts From Within

When the cabin pressure changes on an airplane, oxygen masks drop from the ceiling. What's the first thing that you are told to do? Put on your own mask first. It's pretty simple... you need to be able to breathe in order to help others.

By not taking care of yourself first, you render yourself useless to those around you. The same principle can be applied to your relationship.

If you don't feel that you are largely fulfilled and satisfied with yourself and your own life, it's damn near impossible to make somebody else happy.

You represent half of the people in your relationship. If you want to make your relationship a place where love and communication flows effortlessly, you have to first start by making yourself happier.

Are you currently happy with your life?

Are you living every area of your life according to your highest ideals?

Are you exercising and eating to the point where you have excess energy to burn?

Have you structured several areas of your life around fulfilling your dreams and goals?

Do you surround yourself with friends and social connections that bring out the best in you?

If you were unable to say yes to any of these questions, you need to ask yourself, "Why not?"

Why haven't you given yourself the permission to be happy or feel fulfilled more often than not? It is exclusively under your control to get your own physical and emotional needs met. If you get these needs met outside of your relationship, then you will be bringing a much happier and more fulfilled person into your relationship. Your oxygen mask will be firmly fitted around your mouth, and you will be that much more capable of taking your relationship to the thriving level.

Women often describe that the most attractive men are those who "know themselves." Michael Douglas and Vince Vaughn are examples of men that are by no means traditionally attractive, but have such a self-assured swagger to them that the vast majority of women find them inexplicably attractive. In essence, women are attracted to a man with directionality and confidence.

Directionality is having a committed path or purpose in life. A man with directionality has vision for his future. He has goals and passion; he takes decisive action towards where he aims to head in his life.

Women are attracted to a man who knows himself and goes after what he wants. It's understandable- a man who doesn't know himself or doesn't know what he wants couldn't possibly have gone after *her* unless he wanted her. This gives her certainty in his love for her.

Make intentional efforts towards becoming your absolute best self. Always be on a path of improvement.

Only then can you really be a part of a dynamic, thriving relationship.

# Disclaimer

Although I have written this book for heterosexual males (my primary client base), it can also benefit any person of any gender or orientation, so long as they possess an open mind.

I understand that not every person in the world is in a heterosexual, monogamous relationship. But for simplicity's sake, I have written this book under the assumption that I am addressing a heterosexual man who is currently in a romantic relationship.

I also occasionally use the terms "masculine energy" or "feminine energy." In each case, I use these terms attached to the male and female genders respectively. While doing this, I am fully aware that masculine energy doesn't necessarily belong to the male partner in all situations, nor does the feminine to the woman.

Human beings are dynamic and complex creatures and I acknowledge that, in any given moment, there are thousands of factors at play, all affecting our varying behaviors. No two women are the same, just as no two men are the same.

All of this being said, it is my firm belief that any person of any gender, lifestyle, or sexual orientation can benefit from this book. Before its public release, this book was gifted to friends and family of all walks of life; I have personally seen it rejuvenate and revitalize relationships of only a few months to others of several decades.

Enjoy the book.

# Part 1 - Effectively Expressing Your Love

Most women have a part of them that questions if you still love her just as much as you did when you first started seeing each other. This uncertainty results in a lot of unnecessary arguments that stem from your partner not feeling loved.

She is often looking for clues implicating you are emotionally checked out and she will need reassurance if she finds evidence of emotional disconnect. The right expression of love will help you in establishing and solidifying the emotional relationship that you share.

You might think that she already knows how much you care about her, but that usually is not enough. She wants to hear it. And she wants to hear it often.

Her inner insecurity makes absolute sense. It's actually built into our DNA to ensure our partner's emotional attachment. Evolutionarily speaking, the female partner in any species invests more in the reproductive process because of the risk associated with having children (and this point stands whether or not you have or even *want* children). So your partner is very in tune with whether or not you care for her. She wants as much certainty as possible when it comes to your feelings about her.

As men, we do our best to let our partners know that we care about them and love them. Yet we often hear the common phrases that we "aren't listening" or that we "are being selfish." A gesture that you put time and energy into can quickly get thrown out the door. The end result can be her being upset and you wondering why you even bother.

The small differences between the sexes can be maddening. It's easy to play the blame game and say, "Well, I tried to do something nice but she's just high maintenance, irrational, or crazy."

As I'll go into more deeply over the next several chapters, it is less about what you say or do for your partner and more about *why* you said or did those things. Women pass every one of your words and actions through the filter of "What did that mean?" whereas men tend to take things more at face value.

When there is miscommunication and misinterpretation between you and your partner, everything suffers. You feel uncomfortable around each other. Your moods are affected. Your sex life declines.

If, on the other hand, your compliments and gestures are communicated and interpreted in the way that you intend them to be, communication flows freely, you both feel comfortable, sex is initiated more frequently, and you feel an undeniable sense of connectedness that makes you feel both loved and respected.

You already know how to order flowers, get a gift card to the spa, go out to a fancy dinner, or do any of the other hundreds of suggestions a search engine could offer that would please your partner. What you may not know is that there are far more powerful and effective ways to show your affection. These next chapters will give you the tools to produce far better results than a dozen roses ever could.

In this section, you'll discover what I have found to be the greatest leverage points for bringing the most emotional connectedness to a relationship. Implement just a handful of these and your entire life (not to mention your partner) will benefit.

This book is written from the mindset that small amounts of concerted effort placed in the right parts of your relationship will have the greatest impact on your entire life. But no need to feel overwhelmed! The legwork has already been done for you.

# Power Compliments

*"**B**eing complimented is huge for me. I never really got that from my last boyfriend and sometimes it would get to the point of me asking, "Do you really like me?" I seriously couldn't tell sometimes. So when my current boyfriend tells me how pretty/sexy/amazing I am, it's the complete opposite. And I seriously love it."*

- Laura, 28

Hands down, one of the simplest and most effective ways of making your woman feel more appreciated and loved in your relationship is by giving her a genuine compliment.

You're likely pretty good at giving her compliments, but there is a massive difference between a generic compliment and a Power Compliment. A generic compliment is simply about acknowledging her in some way, whereas a Power Compliment digs deep and really means something.

Generic Compliment: (On the way out to dinner) Wow baby, you look great. Okay, I'm ready. Let's go.

Power Compliment: You are everything I never knew that I needed. You make me a better man and I am so grateful for you in my life.

See the difference?

The first compliment is surface and kind of a throwaway but the second compliment communicates something special. A Power Compliment acknowledges more than just her existence. It expresses appreciation for her effect on you and on your life. It shows that you see her for who she is and it reflects that back to her with truth and eloquence.

Power Compliments take thought and reflecting. They also take the right delivery.

# 1. Coming up with a Power Compliment

The easiest way to start this process is by asking yourself the following questions:

In what ways does she make my life better?

How does she inspire me to be a better person?

What parts of her body drive me absolutely crazy?

How have I grown as a person since we started dating?

What kind of thoughts do I have about her on a regular basis?

Take five minutes right now to reflect on these questions.

To give you some examples, for me and my relationship, the answers would be:

**In what ways does she make my life better?**

- She encourages me to nurture myself, eat well, and exercise regularly.
- She is a ready and willing conversationalist when I need to talk something out.

- She reminds me of who I am when I momentarily forget my path in life.

## How does she inspire me to be a better person?

- She reminds me that I am allowed to slow down and savor moments, and that life is not a race.
- She keeps me motivated in my career when I momentarily doubt myself.
- She encourages me to reach out to my close friends when we have not caught up in a while.

## What parts of her body drive me absolutely crazy?

- I'm crazy about her hips, ass, and thighs.
- I love the dimples on her lower back.
- I love how unbelievably soft her neck is, and how sweet it smells.

## How have I grown as a person since we started dating?

- She has helped me grow into a more aligned version of myself through her encouragement.
- She keeps me accountable with my exercise routine- I am currently in the best shape of my life.
- I have learned to open up more emotionally and love more authentically than I ever have.

## What kind of thoughts do I have about her on a regular basis?

- She is one of the sweetest, and most encouraging women I have ever had the pleasure of meeting.

- I adore the way that her eyes look at me when we are in public.
- How lucky I am to be in a relationship with such an intelligent, beautiful, and nurturing woman.

Now that you've answered the questions for yourself, the next step is to combine, or formulate your notes into Power Compliments.

If you're feeling stuck, I have provided a few more examples of Power Compliments to jumpstart your appreciative and loving mindset. Just remember to use these compliments as a guideline. Because, as always, the best compliments are completely unique to your relationship and are given with total sincerity.

## Looks

- You literally couldn't have been more my physical ideal if I had designed you myself.
- I don't think I actually had a sex drive before I met you… you really bring something out in me.
- Sometimes you look so heart-stoppingly beautiful that I can't concentrate on anything else.
- Have you done something with your… everything? You look radiant.
- Wow… you look absolutely stunning tonight.

## Character and Personality

- You are one of the most loving people I've ever met.
- You have the most attractive mind I've ever known.
- You are so wonderfully loyal to those whom you care about deeply.

- You are one of the most sweet-natured people I've ever known… like Mother Teresa sweet.
- You would be (or are) such an amazing mother.

## Appreciation For What She Brings To Your Life

- I love how encouraging you are from such a genuine place.
- I appreciate how patient and nurturing you are with me.
- The generosity and kindness of spirit that you bring to my life makes every day that much more enjoyable.
- I can't even describe what you bring to my life every single day… but I'm so grateful for it.
- Thank you so much for all of the love and fullness that you bring to my life. I wouldn't be half as happy, productive, or content without you.

## 2. Effectively delivering the Power Compliment

Power Compliments can be delivered many unique ways: by leaving a message in her packed lunch, by emailing her a list of 50 things that you love about her, by hiding a handwritten message in the sun visor of the car (and when you tell her she has a smudge on her face, she is presented with the praise).

Power Compliments can be delivered casually (in bed, over breakfast, etc.) or in more imaginative ways. Think of all of the people, places, and things that she engages with on a frequent basis. Then think about which of those she would least likely expect you to have altered in some way to surprise her with the compliment (like the sun visor example above).

The options are only limited by your imagination.

## 3. Mixing it up

If you are prone to giving her a certain kind of compliment, perhaps concerning her physical appearance, then make a mental note to verbalize your gratitude for her non-physical attributes (for example, her personality, character, values, etc). Conversely, if you primarily give her personality all of the attention, then it's time to praise her physically and sexually.

Just remember that Power Compliments to a woman are like water and sunlight to a seed. Give her the right amount of genuine praise and you will see her blossom.

Practice Power Compliments and I assure you that you will stand out as her best partner.

# Subtle Gestures

*"I get really turned on by the small things in our relationship—how he hugs me in the morning, how he smiles at me when we're holding hands, and even how he puts away my laundry when I don't ask him to. I don't need to hear him say 'I love you' as much as I just need him to show it."*

— Rachel, 41

**There's that saying: big doors swing on small hinges.**

In intimate relationships, very often the small things can have the biggest emotional impact. You know how your partner seems to remember every intimate detail about you and your history together as a couple? There's a reason why she seems to have that super power.

Numerous studies have shown that, in general, male brains tend to have an easier time remembering facts, and figures, while women have an easier time remembering things that are tied to personal relationships (birthdays, anniversaries, first dates, things that you said, things that she said, where you were when certain milestones happened during your relationship, etc.).

Has your partner ever told you that you said something, word for word, a few weeks or a few months after the fact? There is an extremely high probability that she has a better memory of the situation than you do.

**And in terms of subtlety...**

Evolutionary biologists estimate that women are better at picking up on subtleties for a reason. One of my favorite hypotheses is that women (who, for the past several thousand years, have been the primary nurturers of their young) need to be able to read the subtle expressions of their children's moods before they can even speak. Because of this awareness, women pick up on the small things. She appreciates the little gestures that demonstrate your affection.

But the right Subtle Gesture lets her know that she is loved. And the more loved she feels, the more love she'll pour on you.

Men often think that big, expensive dates or lavish gifts are the way to their woman's heart. And while a large-scale gift can have a fantastic return on investment if emotional connection is already established and thriving, they often miss their mark. When it comes to gestures, lots of little ones are better than the occasional grand, sweeping gesture.

# 1. Coming up with a Subtle Gesture

A Subtle Gesture takes listening. So listen to your partner for the next week. Make it a habit to really hear what your partner is talking about and think about some of the following questions while you do so:

– What consistent themes does she bring up?

- Where might she need some encouragement or support?
- What has been stressing her out lately?
- What has she mentioned needing help with?
- What frustrations has she brought up a few times lately?

Make a list of the issues she's been dealing with over the past while and then brainstorm ideas about how you could alleviate stress in her life.

Her dog keeps scratching at the door? Build her a doggy door.

She wishes she could see her siblings more often? Buy a gift card to her favorite restaurant and phone up her siblings to make it happen.

She's been feeling tense lately because of her job stress? Take up a massage course in your free time and give her a surprise rubdown.

Does she seem to enjoy the day-to-day maintenance of the house but resents having to do the household cleaning like vacuuming and dusting? Surprise her by hiring a cleaning service once a month to do all of the heavy duty cleaning for her.

Has she been dropping hints about wanting an adventure? Plan a short weekend getaway for the two of you and tell her in advance so that she can start packing for it.

## 2. Following through with the Subtle Gesture

Though you'll experience some benefit from the Subtle Gesture (the good feeling of making your partner happy), you must not do any of these nice things for her with the expectation that you will be rewarded for it in any way. Even if you are thinking in the back of your mind, "I'm totally going to get _____ for doing this for her," your ulterior motives will be sub-communicated in your actions. This will take away from the power and authenticity of the Subtle Gesture.

Think of what she brings to your life. It's often the details that really affect you the most. Like when she comes up behind you while you're on the computer and runs her fingers through your hair; how she kisses you softly on your face in the morning; the way her eyes sparkle when she looks at you lovingly from across the table. Notice how she doesn't expect anything in return and understand how powerful this makes her actions. If, after each time she ran her fingers through your hair, she immediately asked you to do some chores around the house, you would begin to mistrust her actions. Then, when her fingers met your hair, you would pull away because you would be conditioned to think of this as her way of winning you over to get the chores done. Her actions are more powerful and well received when she doesn't expect anything in return and your Subtle Gesture must be demonstrated in the same selfless manner.

Women have a sixth sense when it comes to being aware of others' intentions (it's called intuition), and she will be able to easily recognize if your intentions aren't in the right place. If she believes that you are doing something nice just to get something in return, then the gesture will fall flat.

And don't get too wrapped up in the process of brainstorming your Subtle Gestures. It can be something as small as pulling out her chair more often, or brushing her hair off of her face.

Just remember: give selflessly! Give with the sole intention of trying to improve your partner's life in the most valuable way possible and your relationship will thrive as a result.

# Calibrated Surprises

*I feel the most loved and cared for when my boyfriend does literally anything that shows that he was thinking of me. Whether it's bringing me a small cupcake because it's my favorite color, doing my dishes while I'm in the shower, or surprising me with sushi after a long day at the office... it all goes a really long way with me.*

- Jennifer, 33

**Women flat-out love being surprised.**

Calibrated Surprises show that you are deeply aware of her and her needs. They demonstrate that you truly care about her. Feeling actively loved for women is like feeling respected and admired for men; it is integral to their internal sense of purpose. Women need to feel loved above all else. It's the way to any woman's heart.

## 1. Creating a Calibrated Surprise

**Start by asking yourself the following questions:**

- What does she value most highly in her life and how can I give her more of it?
- What is something that I could do for her that would help make her life easier?
- When have I seen her the happiest, and how can I create more of those moments for her?
- What things have I done in the past for her that really made her light up with joy?
- Has she ever told me what makes her feel the most loved and appreciated? Have I given her that lately?

Write down at least five answers to each of these questions and then ask yourself "Which three of these things can I do within the next week that will have a positive impact on my relationship?"

It might take a few hours of planning and implementation, but the effect it will have on your relationship will be well worth it.

**If you're looking for some inspiration, check out these five ideas from my personal stash.**

- *Has she mentioned her sore neck/back/legs recently? Set up a candlelit room to give her an hour-long massage (bonus points if you play relaxing instrumental music)*
- *Write her a short poem and leave it somewhere you know she will find it (it's totally fine if it's cheesy and terribly written - just make sure that it rhymes)*
- *If she is leaving on a short trip, pack a small teddy bear into her suitcase as a surprise*
- *Buy her favorite kind of ice cream and put a small note with a Power Compliment on it*

— *Give her a quality gift that is appropriate to her or her hobbies (a new lens for a photographer, a pair of tickets to see her favorite band, etc.)*

The more closely tailored you can make your Calibrated Surprise fit her needs, the better.

## 2. Delivering the Calibrated Surprise

There are two other important components in crafting your Calibrated Surprise.

First, if it's a surprise that you think might be something that she will want some time to adjust to or prepare for, let her know in advance. The romance comes primarily from the fact that you have put forth the time and effort to do something nice for her, and not necessarily from the last-minuteness of the surprise. When in doubt, tell her about the surprise in advance.

For example, if you're planning to surprise her with a date or weekend getaway, you should give her enough time to prepare for it. For a lot of women, having a romantic date night sprung upon them with less than thirty minutes to get ready sounds decidedly unromantic. Ditto for a romantic weekend getaway. And don't even think about trying to pack her bags for her. If you miss one or two essential items, it could very well ruin her weekend.

Second, remember to start small. You don't need to plan a weekend getaway or any other grand sweeping gesture as your first foray into romance. Write a note, send a text, make a meal, buy a rose... just take one small step toward surprising your partner and you'll be simultaneously stepping into your newly thriving relationship.

# Piercing Conversations

*For me, a really good, thorough conversation feels like sex. They are synonymous in my mind. I feel like my partner's attention opens me in the same way that a good night between the sheets does.*
- Rachelle, 27

In the early stages of a relationship, your partner is new and exciting to you. Naturally, you spend a lot more time getting to know each other.

You ask probing questions on dates about her family, values, and childhood. You want to know what makes her come alive in her daily life. You're curious as to whether or not she envisions children in her future.

But after a certain point, conversations for many couples rarely ever penetrate the surface again. The result is that the emotional intimacy in a relationship can all but disappear.

**What is emotional intimacy and why is it important?**

Emotional intimacy comes from knowing the innermost details of your partner's heart and mind. The intangible but obvious feeling of being so interconnected with your partner that you can look into her eyes and know her thoughts. You never have to ask if she's in the mood for sex because you can read it clearly written all over her face. You don't have to spend countless hours of passive-aggressive bickering before you realize that she's upset with you because you're already in tune with who she is and what she's feeling in every moment.

A driving force for boosting a relationship's level of emotional intimacy is something I call Piercing Conversations.

A Piercing Conversation starts with taking interest in her again, giving her the attention that she deserves, and setting aside regular time to have complete alone time with her (phones turned off and all distractions removed).

Brainstorm a list of questions that you want to know about her, but that you never figured out. To get you started, here are some examples of powerful questions you can ask to get a Piercing Conversation rolling:

Who in your life, currently, do you wish you were able to spend more time with?

If you could instantaneously have three new skills, no effort or training involved, what would they be?

What's something that brings you a lot of joy that you wish you had more time for?

Are there any activities that you have wanted to do for a while, but haven't been able to try?

What does your ideal weekend look like?

What little thing have I done in the past few months that made you feel really loved, that I might not have even realized that I did?

If we were to go somewhere new in the world for a week, where would you want to go?

What makes you feel like you've come alive?

Have you ever seen something so beautiful that it made you cry? What was it?

If you were to ask me what my favorite five things about your personality are, what do you think I would say?

As men, we are prone to being overly logical and orderly in our conversations. Women, on the other hand, feel relatively more at ease jumping between different topics. Don't worry too much if the conversation doesn't make too much "sense" to you as you're having it. Your intention is to keep the attentional spotlight on her as much as possible, encourage her to tell you more about herself, and retain as much as you can. And don't worry; we'll get into a lot more communication tips in the next section of the book.

The destination is no destination. The masculine in you will want to bring the conversation to a close… to wrap things up in a neat little package. But your feminine partner doesn't want that in the slightest. She wants to talk, share, and explore. So if you keep focusing on the finish line, you are forgetting to enjoy the journey. The more you find out about her, the better.

## The results of Piercing Conversations are astounding.

Sex comes easier. Unnecessary fights cease to exist. She is your cheerleader and you feel supported by her complete and loving devotion to you.

So if you feel like you and your partner have started to drift apart, or if you feel more like roommates and less like lovers, using this exercise will be a great way to rekindle your emotional intimacy.

# PART 2 - IMPROVING COMMUNICATION

If you haven't noticed already, men and women have very different communication styles- we don't necessarily interpret words and actions in the same ways.

It can be challenging to be aware of this at all times, and it can be challenging to understand what she's trying to communicate. That's why it's so easy to fall into an argument or get into a fight with your partner.

It's critical to improve your communication skills with your partner because fighting is flat-out emotionally exhausting. It affects your ability to perform at work, your ability to focus, your happiness level, and your sex life (if it exists at all during a big fight). As the old saying goes, "Happy wife, happy life."

In the next chapters, I'm going to give you the tools you need to drastically reduce the amount of fighting in your relationship. You will also learn how to effectively connect with your partner when she becomes unresponsive and closed off.

Even if you feel like you don't fight a lot with your partner, you will notice a positive change in your interactions with your partner. She will assume the best in you more often, you will both be less judgmental of each other, and your mutual nagging will cease to exist because your communication will be crystal clear as if for the first time.

By improving your listening skills, taking an encouraging approach, and understanding how to communicate what you're feeling, your relationship will grow exponentially.

But before we get into it, I've had many clients ask me what fighting is and why it can be so intensely draining. A fight is most frequently one of two things. It is either 1) a miscommunication that gets drawn out because each partner is speaking about different things (or the same thing in a different way), or 2) one partner (or both partners!) has an old emotional wound triggered and instead of communicating the hurt, they get defensive and shut down or lash out with anger.

Fights are very different experiences for men and women. For men, it's a feeling of not being respected. For women, it's a lack of connection and not feeling loved. Whatever the differences may be, fights are equally draining for both parties.

Additionally, the very thing that each partner needs the most happens to be exactly what their partner shuts off to them when they feel upset. Men have a tendency to withhold attention during a fight; women, on the other hand, withhold physical affection.

To be clear, each partner isn't necessarily withholding these needs intentionally. Men don't consciously decide, "I'm going to ignore her for the next six hours just to get a rise out of her." Women don't decide, "I'm going to withhold sex for a week and cringe every time he tries to touch me." This withholding is simply an unconsciously occurring byproduct resulting from the unmet needs of each partner.

A man gives love, attention, and affection when he feels a sense of autonomy and mutual respect in his relationship with his partner. But during a fight, a man might feel it necessary to salvage some sense of his independence. As a result, many men retreat into their minds and become largely non-verbal in order to give themselves some space. Nothing could be more frustrating to their partners.

A women gives love, physical affection, and respect to her partner when she feels a sense of emotional connectedness. If a woman doesn't feel loved, she will push you away. Her eye contact is sparse, her communication is terse, and she closes herself off to you physically and emotionally.

I know firsthand how frustrating and exhausting miscommunication can be. But when your energy is being put in the right direction, you will feel a deep sense of respect, connectedness, and love like you never thought possible. These next chapters will take you there.

# Being A Great Listener

For the most part, my clients are *good* listeners. But they often come to me with stories of how they were trying to listen really intently to their partner and she got mad at them for "not listening." Their partners would just stand up mid-sentence and declare, "You don't get it at all!"

It can be frustrating because my clients feel like they are listening. But listening often means something different for women.

Through my coaching over the years, I've picked the top five common listening pitfalls that men make in their relationships.

## 1. Listening and Understanding versus Problem Solving

Men are typically problem solvers. We hear someone is experiencing a challenge and we want to offer a solution. It's hard for us not to! We are like hammers looking for a nail; we are constantly searching for a problem to fix.

So if you're like most men, you've most likely been in the situation where your partner is sharing a problem or challenge with you, and you've offered a solution to help her with the problem only to have her become upset with you.

In these situations, from the male perspective, she was telling you about a problem that needed solving. This is because men commonly communicate with each other in this way. However, from her perspective, she was opening up about something that was meant to bring you closer together. She was sharing something intimate with you.

From the female perspective, being given advice in these situations can feel like rejection. To her, it feels like she was in the process of being open, and vulnerable with you, and you (by giving her advice) told her to "Walk it off. It's nothing." From her perspective, you pushed away her invitation to intimacy by minimizing her story with a simple and dismissive way to "fix" it. But she never wanted you to fix it.

When she says she wants to talk, it doesn't necessarily mean she wants a word-for-word matching dialogue. It usually means she wants you to be witness to her talking while you stay present enough to give her the attention she desires while showing that you want to be there. And guess what? It's actually easier this way. Simply listening and encouraging your partner to talk is the best of both worlds for both parties involved.

She connects to you by telling you what's on her mind- her thoughts, her worries, her hopes, and her frustrations. In her mind, everything that is happening in her life that you don't yet know about feels like a barrier to intimacy. Allow her the chance to tell you about it. Remember that she doesn't need you to sort her life out, or fix her problems; she just wants you to hear her out.

However, every rule has an exception and sometimes she *will* be looking for advice. The only time she wants you to solve her problems is when you feel like her story sharing has shifted. She is no longer simply catching you up on her day. Instead, she is clearly suffering even in the telling of the story and it appears she desires your help in solving this problem.

If you are unsure as to whether or not she wants your advice, wait until she stops talking. Give her five to ten seconds and then ask, "I have something that I think would help that situation, but I'm not sure if that's what you're looking for right now. Do you want me to tell you or would you rather continue sharing your story?"

Asking might be somewhat awkward depending on the situation but it's better to ask and be told "No, just keep listening," than to barge ahead with your solution and get in trouble for it. It's better to be safe than sorry.

## 2. Giving Her The Feedback She Needs

Women are constantly looking for feedback that validates their emotions. They crave validation because by mirroring her feelings to her and showing her that you understand her you are sub-communicating that her feelings matter to you (and by extension, *she* matters to you).

When your partner is sharing her thoughts/stories/life with you, she is looking for a specific kind of listening. We've already established she isn't searching for advice or for you to solve her problems for her. What she really needs is to see attention, comprehension, and empathy from you.

Put simply, she wants to know that you are constantly listening to her, that you understand what she's telling you, and that you are sending her the right type of emotional feedback based on what she is saying.

You might be good at listening and at refraining from sharing your advice, but this is truly the next step in becoming a great listener.

**So how do you achieve this? You *be* her.**

If, during a story, she starts to tell you about a coworker who did something sneaky or manipulative behind her back, and her wide-eyed face is expressing shock, read the emotion on her face and mirror it back to her by saying, "That's insane! How could she have thought that was all right?!"

You want to agree with and validate her emotions, not shy away from them or minimize them. If she feels like you minimize her emotions and her ideas (by stopping the flow of them with advice or worse, by not listening at all), she will stop sharing her emotions and ideas with you. That might sound fun for about ten minutes but you'll quickly realize that her sharing, emotionality, and nurturing style of love will cease to exist along with the conversation.

If she said something awful happened, she wants to hear you say, "That's awful. That must have felt so bad." If something joyful happened, she wants to hear you say, "That's awesome! That sounds like so much fun."

Pay attention to her likes, dislikes, frustrations, milestones, passions, hobbies, and everything else that she chooses to share with you.

You can give supportive feedback to show that you are actively listening in the following forms:

— Softly mirroring her facial movements

- Giving her small verbal feedback
- Asking encouraging and probing questions (for example, How did you feel when that happened? How did that go? What did you do after that?)
- Repeat back parts of sentences that she used in your reply (For example, she's talking to you about how she went shopping with her mom, and you start your question off with "So you went shopping with your mom? How did it go? Where were you shopping?")

While practicing this, you will want to find a balance between actively giving her feedback and passively listening to her. I go into this even more in the final section on sexuality (see Chapter 11 Sexual Polarity).

## 3. Digging Deep

For your partner to really feel like she's being listened to, she'll need to get everything out that she's feeling.

It's up to you, as a great listener and as a great partner, to make sure that she shares everything that's on her mind.

Depending on her mood, this may or may not come easy to her. And more importantly, she'll also purposely leave hints and openings because she wants to test how much you actually care about her. It's up to you to dig deep into these openings. The more you dig, the more it shows that you truly love her.

The openings that she leaves can be short and abrupt, so it's important to pay close attention to her words.

A common example is her coming home from her day of work and describing it as "pretty crazy."

If you reply with "Yeah? That'll happen…" and trail off into watching your favorite sports team, you will leave her feeling unimportant and unloved. She doesn't want to impose her barrage of stories unless you show enough interest that you *want* to hear about them. So it's up to you to dig deep: "Why was it crazy? Come sit down and tell me about it."

It's easy for the male mind to assume that a short response can mean she doesn't want to talk about it. For males, we typically assume that if someone wants to talk about something, they will. It's only logical!

## 4. Listening Between The Lines

How many times has your partner expressed anger over something that seemed inconsequential and small to you?

How about those times when you ask if she's mad and she responds coldly, "I'm fine" when it's clear she's anything but?

Women are generally much better communicators than their male counterparts. One of their major strengths is in using subtext or having a second layer of meaning behind what their words are expressing. That is to say men mean what they say, and women mean what they mean (and not necessarily what they say).

Because of this major difference in communication styles, it's extremely important that you understand and develop your abilities to listen between the lines.

Use your strong analytical and masculine brain to your advantage here. Take the next logical step. If the words she is saying don't make sense, take the next logical step and realize that she's sub-communicating something else to you. Resist coming to the conclusion that she's simply being irrational.

Here are a few examples of how her communication can mean something other than what it may initially seem:

"I'm cold" could mean, "I'm cold, please give me your coat."

"I'm not really feeling like going out tonight anymore" could mean, "I'm feeling disconnected from you emotionally and I want to catch up with you before I feel like going in public."

An exasperatedly expressed "I'm fine" could mean, "I'm not fine and I want you to love me more."

"Fine, if that's what you want to do" could mean, "I don't feel like you're taking my preferences into account."

"You don't care" could mean, "I know that you care about me but I don't feel you have shown it to me in a while. I need you to show me more love."

In the same way that digging deep can show her that you care about her, attempting to understand the subtext of her words can have a similar positive effect. It shows that you care enough and are attentive enough to her emotional needs that you will put in that extra effort to understand what she's really communicating to you.

Learn to see through your partner's words and listen between the lines and she'll feel like no one else on earth has ever understood her as well as you do.

## 5. Fullness of Emotion vs. Emptiness of Emotion

As men, we typically gravitate towards emptiness in our conversations and emotions. We want to figure things out and bring them to a conclusion.

On the flip side, women typically gravitate towards fullness in conversations and emotions. They want to continue connecting through talk.

A common mistake that men make in conversations with their partners is that when they hear their partner is suffering, they try to stop the emotion from happening or they try to redirect it. Though this can be beneficial in certain situations (for example, if your partner has been talking about her stressful day at work for over twenty minutes and you can see she is starting to suffer by re-living it in the process), it is largely unnecessary. It's good to listen to her emotions but you want to ease her back to the present moment if you feel like she is getting lost in the negative emotion of her story.

Imagine that you are at dinner with your partner and you start telling her about your goals in your business life. You would appreciate it if she listened to you for a while, but if you started to get too firmly entrenched in the stress of sharing all of the things you want to accomplish and realizing how far away you feel from achieving these goals, you would appreciate it if she brought you back to the moment with a simple "Have you tried this dessert yet? It is so delicious! Here, have a bite…"

By bringing you back to your senses and out of your head, your partner relieves your suffering. This is the same thing that you can do for her when you feel her slipping too far into her emotional suffering. You bring her back to the present moment by hugging, kissing, or loving her.

It's tempting for men to apply their ways of being onto their partners. It's easy to think, "If I were feeling what she seems to be feeling, I wouldn't want to feel it for very long. I'll help her get rid of those feelings so she can be free from the suffering".

A woman wants to feel free to express herself. She does not want to be limited or restricted in her thoughts or emotions.

Let her hurricane of emotions spin and sit back and take in her feminine energy. When you allow her to experience her emotions in the way she needs to, she will feel respected, seen, and appreciated by you.

# Playing On The Same Team

You want the best for your partner. Therefore, it's only natural that you want her to live up to her full potential.

So why is it that when you make a suggestion to your partner, you are often resented for it?

How you suggest potential change to your partner must be very different than how you communicate it to your male friends.

When your friend John is dragging his heels in his career, you tell him to step up. When Peter is spending money frivolously, you tell him to control himself. They are much more likely to respond to your challenge.

But it's a very different story (and a big mistake) if you tell your girlfriend she should lose weight.

So why do you receive positive feedback when you challenge your friends, but you get in trouble when you challenge your partner?

It comes down to the core of masculine energy versus feminine energy. The masculine in all of us responds to being challenged while the feminine responds to being encouraged.

Assuming that your partner associates primarily with the feminine in your relationship, the reason that she becomes upset with you when you tell her that she is slipping in some way is because you are challenging her in an area where she already feels vulnerable. You are challenging her when you need to be encouraging her.

For a driven man, this can be a difficult concept to understand. If you respond to challenge, it's only natural to assume that others do as well. But not everyone is necessarily as driven and decisive as you are.

You need to learn to lead with praise and not with pressure. You need to learn how to play on the same team.

Do you want to have sex with the lights on more often? Remind her how sexy you find her and actively love and appreciate her body as often as possible.

Do you wish she read more books? Consciously praise her mind and intelligence more than whatever you normally compliment for the next few weeks.

Do you wish she exercised with you more often? Love and appreciate her when she is doing anything remotely active. Tell her how sexy she looks when you see her sweating. Love every part of her body and encourage her throughout her process and you will see the weight drop off.

Encourage, praise, and appreciate whatever actions you want to see occur more frequently.

Speaking of which, how encouraging are you of your self?

A common theme I find with a lot of my extremely driven clients is that they are extremely hard on themselves. I label this state as having a lack of self-love.

If you have a difficult time encouraging your partner, look inwardly first.

One of the best things that you can do for yourself and for your relationship is to practice being more patient, kind, and loving with yourself. Learn to balance the striving aspect of your (masculine) drive with your (feminine) loving and compassionate side. By expanding your ability to love yourself, you give yourself more emotional bandwidth to show love to your partner.

The more you love your so-called imperfections, the more you can appreciate hers.

And while I'm on the subject, have you ever stopped to think about how sexy her imperfections are?

If you think back to all of the hottest/sexiest/most attractive moments in your relationship, they were likely not the ones where your partner was "flawless," but more likely when she was showing herself in her truest, most honest form. As marriage therapist Robert Glover once said, "Humans are attracted to each other's rough edges."

A large element of self-development is the emotional process of getting yourself to a place of believing that you are enough. That you, and how you currently exist, are already perfect as you are. By allowing yourself to ease into that mindset more often, you will find it easier to extend that same kindness to your partner.

In conclusion, if you find it difficult to compliment your partner, it might be because you are being too hard on yourself internally. Every person requires a certain amount of self-compassion and self-love to thrive.

If your mindset is often stuck on challenging, pushing, and growing then you might find it difficult to ease into praising, accepting, and loving. But for the emotional and physical well being of both you and your partner, encouragement and acceptance could be some of the most important actions you ever embrace.

# Respectfully Expressing Your Needs

Men are generally much more limited in their emotional vocabulary compared to women. It's not surprising that men, from a very young age, are encouraged to "toughen up" and express their needs, wants, and feelings very infrequently. The concept that "boys don't cry" is pervasive in Western culture.

So when a man tries to communicate his needs to his partner, it can often be misinterpreted.

As I touched on in Chapter 6, masculine energy gravitates towards emptiness and independence. Men, for the most part, enjoy coming home from work and being able to shut down for a while. Since most men feel like they have to be 'on' at work, it is a very comforting feeling for the masculine to be able to switch off and enjoy their downtime in peace.

However, feminine energy gravitates towards fullness and intimacy. Women, for the most part, enjoy coming home from a day of being away from their partners and catching up. So when she sees you plopping down in front of the television to catch the game, she gets upset with you.

As you can imagine, this dichotomy can cause a lot of unnecessary stress and tension between a couple when the woman wants discussion and connection, while the man wants silence and solitude.

To reduce this stress on the relationship, the best thing you can do is learn how to respectfully express your needs and establish boundaries.

## 1. Getting Your Words Out

Compared to men, women are essentially mind readers. Women can pick up on men's incongruence, vocal inflections, and facial movements with much more relative ease and it can sometimes seem like they are hearing their partner's thoughts. Despite your partner's ability to pick up on most of your subtleties, she isn't actually able to read your mind (Surprise, surprise!).

A woman craves emotional connection with her partner. She often achieves this through communication. But if her communication is momentarily grating to your brain, you must let her know (in other words, of course) so that you can achieve an acceptable balance.

Your masculine mind often tries to go silent in order to numb itself from your partner's words. This doesn't serve either one of you. If you just go quiet and slowly start resenting her in your mind, then you both suffer. She misses out on the emotional connection that she craves, and you don't get the peace and quiet for which you are momentarily desperate. You must take that step in communicating to her to let her know where your head is.

Do you need a few minutes of quiet when you return home from work so you can settle in and feel more ready to talk with her? Tell her.

Do you crave physical touch on a consistent basis, even when it's non-sexual? Let it be known.

## 2. Using The Right Words

In general, the more words you use to express your needs, the better. There is ambiguity in brevity and you might unintentionally offend your partner if you are too short with her. Respectfully tell her what you need, be reassuring, and be a gentleman about it.

For example, if you need some time to yourself after work, you could say, "Baby, I can't wait to hear about your day, especially about _____, but I had a really mentally taxing day at work. Do you mind if I just get ten minutes to myself to breathe and mentally land a bit, and then we can catch up? I would so appreciate that."

Or if you desire her touch, you could tell her, "Few things make me feel more loved and cared for then when you touch me when we aren't about to have sex. Yesterday when you came up and started rubbing my shoulders while I was at my computer I was so happy. I would absolutely love it if you could do things like that more often. It makes me feel really connected to you."

## 3. Continuously Communicating Your Needs

There is no such thing as an entirely autopilot relationship. Your need for independence and her need for intimacy will always be a balancing act. There are some days where you will feel crowded and you will need to take some alone time for yourself, and other days where she will feel disconnected from you and will need some time to catch up.

As men, we are socially conditioned from a young age to believe that relying on others is a sign of weakness, and that to show the cracks in our armor is a bad thing. In reality, few things take more courage and mental strength than letting your needs be known.

By understanding and verbalizing each partner's motivation in any given moment, you can understand her needs and your own needs with much more clarity. This understanding will allow you to avoid fights that truly stem from nothing. Getting your emotional vocabulary and communicative awareness to a higher level will do away with 90% of the fights that you are currently experiencing in your relationship (with your soon-to-be empowered sex life doing the rest of the work- see Part 4: Supercharging Your Sex Life).

Even if it feels scary sometimes, communicating your needs and desires within your relationship will always benefit you. You are used to pushing yourself in other areas of your life; now it's time to start pushing yourself to become comfortable in effectively expressing your needs.

# Part 3 - Taking the Lead

Taking the lead in your relationship is a key component in making it thrive. Intentionally striving and pushing to make yourself, your partner, and the relationship better benefits everyone.

Why is leading so powerful? Women want to feel your masculine strength. They want to feel your emotional and psychological boundaries at all times. It ignites her passion for you when you are able to witness her emotions without necessarily taking them on as your own.

If you can show that you can handle yourself and lead confidently in a variety of situations across your relationship, then she will feel an even deeper sense of trust in you.

Remember, women respond to your masculine directionality (or leadership ability) just as much as you respond to her feminine nurturing (love). Examples of feminine nurturing: how she gently strokes your arm while you drive, nourishes you with food when you accidentally skip a meal, or places your head on her chest before you leave your shared bed in the morning on your way to work.

Examples of masculine directionality: encouraging her to follow her dreams, physically leading her through a crowded room, and simplifying a problem in her mind that eases stress from her life. Give each other your gifts and don't hold back.

Leading is often perceived as a negative quality in a society that values community and fairness. The reality is that being decisive can be very loving and nurturing when done properly.

Telling her how she feels about something, asking her to lose weight, or demanding that she make you a meal is not being a leader. It's being a domineering jerk.

By leading in a firm and kind way, you are demonstrating through your actions that you value your time with her, and it shows that you are intentional about the relationship. Women love seeing the thought and effort that goes into your actions. It isn't necessarily the act themselves, but what it means that matters. Showing how much you care about her is what's most important.

# Being a Loving Leader

*I love a man who can lead confidently without being overbearing about it. For me, the more effort he puts into the date, the more perfect it is. I can put up with a certain amount of 'So what do you wanna do...' conversations, but I would really rather not!*

- Kiran, 24

Learning to be a leader in your relationship takes practice and a good understanding of the balance that needs to be maintained.

Lead too aggressively and you come across as overbearing. Lead too softly and you seem unable to lead with your meager masculine energy.

## 1. Finding Balance Between Firmness and Kindness

One of the keys to being a Loving Leader is to always lead with firmness and kindness. You aren't simply leading to be seen as a leader, you are encouraging her to do things that you know will help her grow.

## What does too firm look like?

1. Telling her to lose weight
2. Motivating her with intense challenges
3. Demanding that she do a favor for you (make you food, do the laundry, etc.)

## What does too kind look like?

1. Asking her what she wants to do for all of your date plans (instead of planning something yourself)
2. Never having preferences for what the two of you have for dinner
3. Never initiating sex because you only want to do it when she is the one who is really in the mood

## What does the right balance look like?

1. Physically leading her to her chair in a restaurant
2. Encouraging her to try a new activity that she once thought was out of her comfort zone
3. Encouraging a discussion on something in her life that makes her feel vulnerable (her body, her career, or her relationship with her parents)

The directionality and leadership ability of your masculine side allows her to feel safe enough to try these challenging activities. After she tries them and succeeds, her trust in you increases.

Why does she feel safe with your leadership ability? Imagine that feminine energy is a tornado, and that masculine energy is a giant rock on the ground. The ever-changing, fluid style of the tornado takes comfort in knowing that there is something as heavy and consistent as the rock. You are the rock that she takes solace in. She revels in your weight and consistency, just as much as you enjoy her movement and unpredictable nature.

By the way, when I talk about your consistency I don't mean the consistent externalities of your life (your fitness level, your current job, your wardrobe, etc.). I'm talking about the consistency in your character, values, and what kind of experience she is able to have whenever she is around you.

Being a leader doesn't have to be all about grand sweeping gestures. The little things count just as much.

Plan dates. Pull out chairs. Open her car door for her. Give her suggestions at a restaurant when she's unsure of what to order and you know what she generally likes. Book a cooking course for you two to take together.

The details often count more than the grand gestures, so start small and see where it takes you.

## 2. Making Future Plans

While many men fear discussing the future with their partner, you don't have to be 100% certain of your future to talk about future plans with her. Nothing is certain in life. But if you are committed to her now, you have to talk from that place. If you "play it safe" by holding back from expressing your true desires then she will feel as though you are lying to her (because, in that moment, you will be holding back your truth and, therefore, lying). So tell her what you think of her, tell her often, and commit to talking about your future together- whatever that may look like.

By making and verbalizing plans together for the future, you show that you have the strength to not need to be the only one who has input. You are showing the strength of leading, while maintaining the sensitivity of flexibility.

Mention that you would love to travel to Italy with her next year. Ask if she's ever wanted to try rock climbing and start looking up locations for the two of you to learn it. Figure out what goals you both have uncrossed on your respective bucket lists and decide how to make your potential, 'one day' plans a reality together.

By taking the initiative to make plans with her, especially long-term plans, you show that you are committed to her. You show that you are already thinking about a future together. This is so key for women as they need trust, connection, and intimacy in order to fully relax with you and open up in the relationship.

# Opening Her Emotionally

Just as men are often pressured to be strong, stoic and fearless, women are often pressured to be levelheaded, rational and calm.

If you've ever told your partner to "calm down," "relax," or "stop being so sensitive", then you already know she doesn't react well to it.

Think about how it feels when you are told to "man up," or to "stop being a baby." It doesn't feel good, does it?

The danger of this societal suppression is that, when women are told to bite their tongues, they are learning to numb themselves emotionally. They grow to distrust their emotional intuition. They hold back from telling their partners their true feelings because they fear that they will come across as nagging or overly critical.

Women feel as though the way they are in their real, uncensored moments is in some way wrong and so they suffer. Meanwhile, men suffer without the emotional mirror (their partner) that helps them through their darker days.

Your woman's greatest gift is the endless depth and intuition that she has in her power to help you become the best man possible. By learning how to help open your woman so that she can relax into her truest self, you will both benefit. She will feel seen and appreciated for who she truly is- as if for the first time.

## Why She Closes

She closes when she's had a rough day at work, or when she finds herself less attractive, or when she feels unappreciated. She closes for thousands of reasons, but primarily she closes when she doesn't feel loved. She closes because she wants to see if you will notice and care enough to open her up again.

When she seems to be emotionally closed off to you and it seems as though she is suffering, it's up to your masculine side to lovingly encourage her to open up to you. Your masculine energy reassures her to come back to a place of love and contentment. Just as you would want your partner to call you on anything demonstrating a lack of integrity ("You said you would complete this task by this time, and you didn't."), you can do the same for her.

## How To Open Her

When your woman feels closed off to you, she needs to feel your strength. She wants to know that you will be able to handle whatever she throws at you. And until she feels confident that you will be able to handle her, she will hold back.

But you have to push through. And you have to *want* to push through.

There are three main ways I tell clients to open their woman.

## 1. Ask

Ask her to talk to you.

"What's going on?"

"Can you tell me what kinds of things you're feeling?"

"Are you feeling all right? It seems like something has been on your mind for the past few hours/days."

Ask and you shall receive. Whether or not she can verbalize what is happening for her, your inquiry shows that you are taking the time to notice her. By demonstrating that you both recognize and care about what is happening with her, you are taking the first step in unwinding the tension that has been stored inside of her.

Make sure that you are asking her what's wrong from a place of calm, genuine interest. If she senses your frustration with her, she could shut down even further (as she could perceive your frustration as anger).

So what tone should you be approaching your partner with? Imagine how you would speak to a five-year-old version of your partner after she falls and skins her knee. A mix of patience, compassion, love, tenderness, and concern would be present in your tone. It is this same balance that you are looking to achieve when bringing your partner out of her emotional closure.

## 2. Listen

Listen, and only listen.

Don't problem solve, minimize her situation, or tell her how she should feel.

Simply listen with an open mind, open ears, and an open heart and she will let you know where she is (see Chapter 5 Being a Great Listener).

### 3. Love

If your partner is feeling unloved, then the antidote is pressing your love onto her.

She may resist your initial attempts to reconnect but this is merely the feminine's energetic resistance. It isn't that she's trying to make sure that you know you messed up; it's simply that she wants to make sure you are still loving her. She needs to know that you care enough about her to push through her resistance.

Encourage her through her rough spot. Tell her how brave, strong, and powerful you see her being.

Stare deeply into her eyes, hold her tightly against your body, and kiss her like you mean it. Show her that you love her. Be patient and persistent with her opening.

## The Proactive Approach

Your partner doesn't just need the right actions from you; she also needs you to be proactive in your awareness of her emotions. It's one thing to be in a reactive state in which you only pay attention to her when you feel her suffering, and quite another to be proactively aware of her at all times.

While you aren't responsible for her emotions or moods, you do want to give her the certainty that you will always be a sounding board for her thoughts, and that you will always be a safe space in which she can open.

You can achieve this during any point of your relationship (but the sooner, the better). Simply let her know that she is safe by sharing something along these lines- "I hope you know that I will always be here for you. If you've had a bad day and want someone to listen to you, or you feel less than attractive and need some extra love, or whatever comes up on any given day... I want you to always feel like you're safe with me. You don't ever have to hold back with me. I want real transparency between us."

Transparency is sexy.

# Getting Over Arguments & Apologizing

Arguments and disagreements are nothing short of draining. They affect your mood and ultimately your ability to perform in other areas of your life. It's especially taxing when the fallout of the argument lasts for an entire day or longer.

The majority of the time, arguments arise from a simple miscommunication. The issue at hand can be so inconsequential but it is somehow allowed to take over your world.

Maybe you have had a hard time making it to the gym lately and so you make a comment about how you would love it if your partner went to the gym with you more often (which would help keep you accountable and make you stay on a more consistent schedule). She takes offense and accuses you of telling her that she is out of shape. What was already a potentially vulnerable request on your behalf is being attacked; you shut down because fighting over something so stupid feels irrelevant. Within seconds, you wish you hadn't brought up your concern. As a result, you become less likely to want to ask for help in the future.

The biggest misconception I see from my clients is that apologizing is a sign of weakness.

The truth is, the *inability* to apologize makes you appear weak to your partner. It sub-communicates that you can't handle someone looking through the cracks in your armor.

But the "Alpha male" is a concept of the past. Strong, confident, community-minded leaders are taking over the world as the more heavy-handed rulers of the past fall to the wayside- and for good reason. Your partner doesn't want you to stubbornly push ahead and pretend like you did nothing wrong. She wants you to be strong-minded but egoless enough to admit that yes, you are a human, and yes, you made a mistake.

Apologizing is not compromising your value or integrity. Apologizing is honest and authentic. Refusing to apologize (especially when you know you are in the wrong) is stubborn and emotionally guarded.

Women often hear communication from their partner through the lens of "Am I being loved right now?"

Men often hear communication through the lens of "Am I being challenged right now?"

We all make mistakes in our relationships (we are only human) and it's critical that we know how to effectively and thoroughly apologize for those mistakes.

The beautiful thing about apologizing in a leading way is that there is everything to gain: having a greater sense of integrity, experiencing character growth, maturing emotionally, and relying less on ego-based thinking. Being seen as more attractive to your partner and making her happier aren't bad side effects either.

There are five simple steps that I've outlined to put an argument to rest so that you may get back to a place of harmony in your relationship.

## 1. Acknowledge Your Mistake Specifically

For the male brain, arguments typically fall under 3 categories: she's wrong, I'm wrong or we're both wrong.

First of all, as tempting as it would be to think otherwise, it is very rare that she is 100% in the wrong and that you shoulder 0% of the blame. The blame game isn't a fun one to play, but if you look at your argument through a clear lens, it is highly likely that you had at least *some* input into the miscommunication. If it so happens that she *is* entirely responsible for the argument, take the high road. Don't feel the need to make an example of her - that's simply your ego speaking. There is a huge amount of strength in not needing to say, "I told you so."

If you think you might have messed up but you can't figure out exactly what you've done to upset your partner, take a look at Part 2 on Communication Styles. Focus on Chapter 5 Being A Great Listener, and specifically on Listening Between The Lines.

The bottom line is that, in the resolution of any argument, you have to acknowledge the fault as specifically as possible.

Whether you forgot to pick up your kids, or you accidentally insulted her parents, or you left the cheese out, acknowledge it. Tell her, "Hey, I have to talk to you about something. Yesterday when I (did/said _____), I feel like I really messed up."

## 2. Express Remorse For The Act

Show that it's affecting you and you feel bad about it. The reason for this is that when something that you do causes her emotional distress, she wants to know that it registers on your radar.

If you feel any combination of shame, fear, embarrassment, vulnerability, sadness, or regret, then it's best to let her know. The more information she has about your emotions, the better. Again, letting her know that you are *feeling* remorse and not just *thinking* that you should feel remorse are entirely different things.

Say, "That really isn't the kind of guy that I'm trying to be and I feel terrible about having (done/said ____)".

## 3. Recognize And Validate Her Feelings

Let her know that you're aware of her in this process. When most guys apologize, they only speak about themselves and their intentions.

They say things like:

"I wasn't trying to hurt you."

"I didn't mean to show up late to our date."

"I wish I hadn't done that."

But she isn't looking for you to explain yourself. She wants to know that you understand how your actions affected *her*.

If you're just apologizing to clear your conscience, she will be able to pick up on it.

To validate her feelings, you want to say things like:

"That must have been very frustrating to be sitting by yourself for twenty minutes, I'm sorry that I made you wait so long."

"I know you must have felt anxious when I didn't call. I would have felt anxious too."

"I'm sorry if you felt abandoned when I fell asleep during the middle of your story. That was not respectful of me and that couldn't have felt good for you on any level."

So how do you combine these first three steps?

Say something along the lines of, "I feel like my (actions/words) might have made you feel (hurt/excluded/offended/etc.) and I'm sorry if I made you feel that way. I know that I would feel (hurt/excluded/offended/etc.) if I were in the same situation and that couldn't have felt very good."

## 4. Tell Her Your Plans For Error Correction

This point is the first step in the one-two punch that really makes this process knockout your arguments. Telling her your plans to change in the future is powerful, and it really gets taken to the next level when combined with step 5.

If you say something along the lines of, "I can tell that I've messed up and I don't want this to happen again. I will make sure this doesn't happen by doing _____ instead in the future." This gives her the reassurance that you truly understand what you did wrong and that you are consciously trying to prevent it from happening again.

## 5. Do Something About It

This is the most important step.

Generally, women don't live nearly as much in the contextual world of time and space as compared to men. They are much better at being present minded.

Promising, "I won't do this ever again" isn't necessarily powerful because you aren't showing anything in that current point in time.

In the moment that you are apologizing and only saying that you won't do it again, she will still feel her trust being hurt. The feminine is much more present minded ("I feel hurt right now") whereas the masculine is more contextual in its thinking ("We have barely had sex this month"). When, in the present moment, your partner feels like she's been lied to, she closes off to you. She shuts down and puts up a wall between the two of you to make sure that you care enough to break through it.

Therefore, the most important thing to do after you verbalize your apology is to take action. You have to show that you learned a lesson and that you are doing something about it.

The action needs to be specific to the situation for it to be powerful. While buying her flowers or taking her out for a nice date won't hurt, it won't be nearly as amazing as if you had planned something particularly calibrated to the offense at hand.

If you hurt her sister by saying something that was inadvertently offensive, then your action step would be to call her sister and apologize to her personally.

If your partner's trust in you has been compromised because you said you would do something and then you forgot or chose not to do it (mow the lawn, attend the ballet with her, etc.), then do the thing that you committed to do.

Did you say that you would take her out for a nice meal to celebrate a minor milestone and then you forgot? Better get on the phone and make a reservation.

This may seem overwhelming, but each step is simple (in fact, you might already be doing a few of them without thinking about them). Remember, set your ego aside, become adept at apologizing when you need to, and you will remove so much unnecessary stress and resentment from your partner's life as well as your own.

# Part 4 - Supercharging Your Sex Life

How confident do you feel in your current sex life with your partner?

You have an idea that your partner is probably enjoying herself by the sounds that she makes when she's with you, but you know that not all orgasms are created equal. You want to make sure that you are bringing the heat in the bedroom.

For a lot of my clients, the sexual components of their relationship is an area where they have the most room to learn and grow. As men, we typically don't develop an extensive vocabulary around sex, nor do we necessarily have a comprehensive understanding of the physical side of sex. We don't talk about this stuff in any real detail with our male friends. You have to dig deep in weird tantra books that have intricate (and often confusing) drawings and all too frequently, the information that we receive regarding sex is incomplete and falsified.

It's important to realize that while sex and physical intimacy are an integral part of a thriving relationship, they aren't everything. Relationships are made up of emotional connection, sexual intimacy, and a willingness to help free your partner to allow her to become the best possible version of herself. The previous chapters will get your emotional connection to a place it's never been (which will also affect, to some extent, your sex life). This section of the book will focus entirely on the sexual side.

It's also important to realize that, in order to have the best relationship possible, you have to maintain the right balance of these components.

An intimate relationship is a constant balancing act between increasing and decreasing your emotional and sexual energy. It would be just as inappropriate for you to start taking off your pants in the middle of your partner sharing her stressful day as it would be to start telling her about your childhood emotional issues in the middle of intercourse. It's imperative that you know how and when to slide up or down either emotional or sexual intimacy, and I will get into this extensively in the following chapters.

# Sexual Polarity

The first step in supercharging your sex life is finding the right balance of emotional and sexual connection with your partner in everyday life.

By developing the awareness and ability to shift the dynamic of your relationship in any moment, you will always be able to give her exactly what she needs from you.

You've most likely experienced different levels of sexual polarization at different times in your relationship. There were likely moments when you weren't sexually attracted to your partner at all (when you were fighting, for example) and others when you couldn't keep your hands off of her. Generally, though, any given relationship hovers around an average set point. It's in your hands whether or not you want increase emotional, or sexual attraction from that set point in any given moment.

In a low sexual polarity relationship, couples connect well emotionally and tend to describe each other as their "best friend." But their sex life is usually infrequent and dispassionate.

In a high sexual polarity relationship, the sex is lightning-bolt-to-the-crotch amazing. You can slam each other against the wall at any time of the day and have hot, passionate sex. But when not engaged with each other sexually, your emotional connection and ability to communicate with each other has a tendency to suffer.

The ideal situation is for your relationship to be dynamically sexually polarized.

When you are relaxing together and engaging in conversation, you can depolarize yourselves to a low-polarity state so that it is easier to connect with each other emotionally. But when things start heating up sexually, you know how to dial up the sexual charge to increase your mutual desire. It has the benefits of both low-polarity and high-polarity relationships.

Having emotional connection and sexual attraction are not mutually exclusive- it's not an either/or scenario. Connection and attraction are to be interwoven within your relationship because what she needs from you in any moment will always be changing.

## When To Increase Emotional Connection

Increase emotional connection whenever your partner wants to talk. Maybe you find yourself asking "Why is she telling me this?" anytime she starts talking to you about something seemingly irrelevant. Understand that she is telling you these things because it makes her feel more connected to you by having shared them.

For example, after coming home from work, she tells you some run-of-the-mill stories about her co-workers, some tasks that she completed, and her delicious lunch. During the telling of the story her mood alternates between happy, excited, neutral, and bored.

In this scenario, she needs emotional connection. She needs your softer side to listen to her. She is telling you about all of these things because she wants to establish the emotional connection of you knowing about her day. She is not looking for any problems to be solved- she just wants to feel listened to (see Chapter 5 How To Be A Great Listener).

## When to Increase Sexual Polarity

Increase sexual polarity with your partner anytime you feel your partner needing to be broken out of her stress, frustration, or anxiety.

For example, after coming home from work, she tells you about one of her co-workers who was absolutely horrible to her during her coffee break. She mentions a report that she accidentally delivered to the wrong mailbox and how she spent half of her day chasing it before it got into the wrong hands. And to top it all off, her employer threatened to fire her if she didn't stop coming in late (but her car broke down on the way to work and she couldn't have planned for that).

In this scenario, she needs to borrow from your strength. She has gone from a place of sharing to a place of suffering. As she continues to tell you about her day, you can see her eyebrows furrowing more and her heart and mind are suffering. She needs to be able to fall into your strength. She needs to be taken into your arms and be held. She wants to hear, "That sounds awful! But it's over now. Come here and lay your head on my chest."

# How To Increase Sexual Polarity

## 1. Work Out Hard

Go to the gym more often to connect with the animalistic side of your masculine energy. By doing so, you connect to the same mental state that links sex to aggression. This inner beast is perfectly healthy to make friends with.

You know the face that you make when you are on your last rep and you growl because you feel like capturing and killing your dinner? That's the primal side of your masculine energy surfacing. By tapping into this inner beast, you tap into your sexual energy. Working out hard allows you to connect with your primal self on a regular basis, making it easier to tap into that animalistic energy in the bedroom with your partner.

If you have been working a desk job for years and exercise has fallen off of your to-do list, this tip alone will reinvigorate your sex life tenfold.

## 2. Express Your Sexual Attraction

Women want to feel seen as a sexual being by their partner. Your romantic partner is not just your friend that lets you sleep with her. She wants to feel feminine around you. She is your lover. So treat her as such.

See her walking up the stairs? Chase her up them. Is she doing the dishes? Come up behind her and envelope her with your arms, or smack her bum playfully, or nibble her on the neck. Lying on the couch together watching a movie? Grab her beautiful hip while you let out a little growl.

She should rarely be able to walk past you without a kiss.

If you want to keep the sexual simmer going, you have to bring the heat.

## 3. Take Charge

If you really want to turn up the sexual energy quickly, physically dominate her in subtle (and not so subtle) ways.

The feminine in your partner responds to the qualities in you that could be described with one word: leader. When you combine your calm, confident, and flexible leadership ability with your dominant sexual energy, your partner will go crazy for it.

Pin her down on the bed. Push her arms against the wall and kiss her deeply. Stare into her eyes with a penetrating gaze and let the beast that you connected with in the gym start to slide into your stare.

# How To Increase Emotional Connection

Read and implement the first ten chapters of this book!

Remember that sexual polarity and emotional connection are about loving your partner in the way that she needs you to love her in any particular moment.

Sometimes she needs your strength, and sometimes she needs your soft side. Learn to read her, and give her what she needs.

No matter what kind of relationship you have, as long as you are staying aware of your partner and putting in the work, maintaining a thriving, active-polarity relationship is completely possible.

# Power Compliments

When I ask my clients if they want to be the best sexual partner that their wife or girlfriend has ever had, their eyes light up with excitement. Everyone wants to be their partner's best sexual partner. It is hardwired into our competitive male brains to want to be the best at everything, and this includes our sex lives.

In order to understand how you can be your best in lovemaking, it's first important to understand that men and women experience sex in somewhat different ways.

Both partners see sex as connection. Women, more often than men, want sex in order to know that her partner still finds her desirable. She finds solace in your initiation of sex because it shows your attraction to her. Men, more often than women, experience sex as their primary means of connecting. Men want sex to determine whether or not they have sexual access to their partner. Conversation is great and all, but if you don't feel that your partner is sexually available to you, you shut down pretty quickly.

Just as a lot of your sexual self-esteem comes from the idea that you need sexual access to her, much of your partner's comes from knowing that you are still very much attracted to her.

Because sex is such an emotional process, she wants to feel safe, secure, and sexy around you. You can increase your partner's feelings of safety, security and sexiness by demonstrating to her, both verbally and physically, how much you adore and appreciate her from a sexual standpoint.

Sex will come easier, she will initiate sex more than she currently does, and she will feel more comfortable pushing sexual boundaries with you if she feels safe and attractive.

# Praising Her Sexually - Verbally

As much as it may seem like it at times, women are not mind readers. It might seem good enough to you that you complimented her body, face, or sexual ability more at the beginning of your relationship, but your partner wants to hear how you feel about her frequently.

As a rule of thumb, tell her five times more than you think she wants to hear your praise in an ideal world. You think she wants a compliment on her hair/bum/stomach/face/clothing a few times a week? Multiply that by five!

And don't just verbalize your appreciation for the obvious things; compliment her on the details that you notice about her. Compliment the things you know she feels self-conscious about. Does she even know what your favorite part of her body is? Make her aware!

If you don't know where to start, here are a few ways you can begin to verbalize your sexual praise:

- You look absolutely stunning.
- You have the sexiest bum I have ever seen.
- I love how your hair smells.
- I love this little curve in your lower back- it gets me every time.
- You have such an adorable little nose.
- You look so sexy when you come home from the gym and your face is still red.
- You have the most beautiful face I've ever had the pleasure of kissing.
- Your thighs are so delicious, I could eat them.
- Sometimes you look so sexy that I think I might pass out (and this is one of those times)!
- You have such a radiant smile.

As always, whatever is the most calibrated to what you actually like about your partner is ideal. She will feel the sincerity behind your words before you even finish your sentence if you do this right.

Let her see you being affected by her beauty. Don't try and play it cool. Let your beast out. Show her how much you want to ravish her with the way that you look at her while you praise her sexually.

You are her partner. She won't think it's creepy, she will absolutely adore it. So start today. If she's close to you now, tell her your favorite things about her physical appearance. Be generous with your verbal praise.

## How To Praise Her Sexually - Physically

The other way that you can show her how much you adore her is through touch.

If you touch her like she's your partner of several years and you're simply going through the motions, she will feel that intention behind your touch. She will know where your heart and mind are by the way that you touch her.

But if you touch her like it's the first time you've ever touched a woman's body, she will feel that too.

Let your hands and mouth roam the length of her body. Envelope her with your touch. Savor her.

How would you touch her if this were the last time you would ever be with a woman? That's how you want to be touching her on a daily basis.

In the way that you look at, talk about, and touch her body, let her know that it affects you deeply and that you adore it. This is never something that you need to hide.

I know that it can seem a little nerve-racking, letting her know just how greatly you are attracted to her. It might have started when you were young and you were taunted for your schoolyard crushes (Jimmy likes Susie! Jimmy likes Susie!). Or maybe your hesitation stems from the first time you ever asked out a girl and she harshly rejected you. Whatever the root cause, many men never get over the fear of expressing their likes and desires openly when it comes to women. But there is nothing more natural for human beings than sexual desire. It has kept us alive and well for thousands of years. Sexual desire is a powerful force that deserves to be expressed uninhibitedly.

Let loose your appreciation for your partner and she will thank you for it in her own way (and trust me, it's a good way).

# Pleasuring Her Physically

There seems to be, with the majority of my clients, only a basic, "fuzzy" understanding concerning how to truly physically pleasure their partners. And unless you have sought out books or taken courses on sexual techniques and theories, it's likely a subject that's a little bit fuzzy for you as well.

In this chapter, I want to arm you with the base knowledge and understanding of the female sexual anatomy so you can feel confident in your ability to pleasure your partner sexually. Because when you and your partner are feeling sexually satisfied with each other, the unnecessary fights stop, your confidence soars, and your relationship is that much more fulfilling and connected.

Please also keep in mind that I've taught several 20-hour live courses on sexual mastery for men. If you need more help with this, contact me for coaching.

Sex is much deeper than simply getting her sufficiently wet enough for you to put your penis inside her. Sex is a transformative tool that, when executed properly, connects you to your partner more deeply than anything else. Conversation and praise wish they had the same level of power as passionate sex does in a relationship.

## P.E.L.V.I.C.

PELVIC is a go-to acronym I use for what makes sex a complete and satisfying experience for women:

**P**resence
**E**motion
**L**asting
**V**ariety
**I**ntensity
**C**ontrol

**Presence** refers to how present you feel to her. Does it seem like you are in your head and trying to pull off some technique that you read about in a men's magazine as opposed to actually being aware of her? Then you will not come across as present.

Forget how you think you *should* be pleasuring her, and pay attention to how she is responding to you, moment to moment. Be generous with your eye contact and listen to every bit of feedback she gives you.

**Emotion** is an undeniably integral part of having sex with your partner. Part of staying present with your partner is showing her how she affects you emotionally. Whether that emotion is desire, appreciation, love, or lust, let it show without censoring it. Your sex life is the place for you to let it all hang out and be the most honest version of yourself possible.

**Lasting** in bed means different lengths of time to different people. Some women can achieve orgasm in under two minutes, while other women take over 20 minutes to climax. The vast majority of men ejaculate in under three minutes from penetrative intercourse and because of this, most women don't experience penetrative orgasms with their partners.

Every man has had difficulties with premature ejaculation at some point in his life. Over 30% of men who suffer from chronic P.E. last anywhere from 15-60 seconds (many don't even make it to penetration). If you are going to help your partner achieve a penetrative orgasm, it is imperative that you learn to delay your orgasm and help her reach hers before you both climax (more on this in the following chapters).

**Variety** is the spice of life- and this doubles when it comes to your sex life. If you are doing it right, sex with the your partner is never the exact same experience. You can learn to go deeper and deeper into your sexual selves and push each other's sexual boundaries to see what you both desire and are capable of.

**Intensity** is the collective strength, power, and presence that you bring to your sexual experiences. Your partner needs you take her and ravish her open during some of your sexual encounters. If your sexual endeavors are explorative, drawn-out evenings filled with laughter and emotional connection, that's not necessarily a bad thing, depending on your partner… but if that's all you are capable of giving her? She might need you to step up the sexual polarity once in a while.

**Control** is your ability to lead your sexual experience with your partner. Whether that means bringing her to climax or delaying your ejaculation, physically putting her in different positions, or knowing when to dial up or down the sexual polarity, it is essential to stay aware of her and her emotional needs throughout the entire process. Control is being able to calibrate your actions to what your partner needs in each moment and it is necessary for a deeply fulfilling sexual experience.

## The 3 Types Of Vaginal Orgasms

Women have the advantage over men when it comes to the variety of sexual pleasure they are able to receive (not to mention the ease with which women can have multiple orgasms compared to most men). While most men only have one option for the kind of orgasm they can have with their sexual organs, women possess three types that can be induced. Unfortunately, due to the lack of quality sex education in a lot of the developed world, most people (men and women) are unaware of this fact.

The key to helping your partner achieve any of the three types of orgasms (and to being a mind-blowing lover in general) is to be a good listener. If you really listen to her and pay attention to how she is responding to your touch, you'll be much better at easing the sexual pressure on or off in any one moment.

### 1. Clitoral

Clitoral orgasms are generally the easiest to achieve and are a relatively introductory orgasm compared to the other two orgasms.

The clitoris has roughly double the amount of nerve endings than those found in the entire penis. Its sole function is to act as a pleasure button for your partner; therefore, it can be extremely sensitive at times, especially when she is first starting to become aroused.

The clitoris responds well to sameness. Once you have found a motion that your partner enjoys (any combination of up-and-down, side-to-side, squeezing, or licking), keep the same rhythm and pressure until she orgasms or seems like she is becoming too sensitive (in which case, you may need to slow down or change the motion or pressure).

Clitoral orgasms have a similar build-up, peak, and resolution cycle as a deeply satisfying sneeze. And similar to sneezes, many women are able to have multiple clitoral orgasms in one night of lovemaking (but don't touch it right after she comes as it is often much too sensitive to touch for a few seconds/minutes afterwards).

If you are unsure as to how your partner prefers to have her clitoris stimulated, ask her to masturbate for you briefly. Pay close attention to how she touches herself. Does her hand move primarily side to side, up and down, or in circles? How light or firm is her touch? Then, mirror her movement, matching the direction, pressure, and pacing with your mouth or tongue and pay attention to her response. Remember the key word for being a great lover: listen.

Once she has reached a clitoral orgasm, her labia will be engorged and her vagina will be much more receptive to further stimulation (making it easier for her to achieve the next two types of orgasm).

## 2. G-Spot

The G-Spot produces a more powerful and fulfilling orgasm than the clitoris does. This orgasm can also cause the woman to ejaculate. (Don't worry; it's not pee.)

The G-Spot (also known as the Grafenberg spot) is a quarter-sized area located one to two knuckles deep inside the vaginal canal on the anterior (stomach side) wall. The G-Spot has been studied for decades but its existence has been debated- likely by men who couldn't locate it within their partner.

To stimulate the G-Spot, insert one or two fingers into the vagina and make a beckoning motion. Similar to the clitoris, you want to start off somewhat softly, slowly adding more pressure and intensity to your fingers over the course of several minutes. It can take anywhere from two to twenty minutes to achieve a G-Spot orgasm through manual stimulation so make sure your forearm is up for the challenge (and your partner is comfortable and as relaxed as possible).

G-Spot orgasms can also trigger a much bigger uprooting of emotion for the recipient so consider yourself warned that your partner might laugh, cry, or shake uncontrollably for a few minutes during/after her orgasm. Whatever you do, stay with her and keep that safe bubble around her. If she starts crying and you freak out and put physical or emotional distance between the two of you, she will trust you less and your sex life (and relationship) will suffer for it. She will only ever give you what she thinks you are able to handle. Show her that you have the mental strength and maturity to handle whatever she throws at you and your mutual sexual satisfaction will benefit.

## 3. Cervical

Cervical orgasms are the most soul-altering type of vaginal orgasm that women are capable of achieving.

Cervix literally translated from its Latin origin means "the neck of the womb." The cervix is located at the deepest part of the vagina and marks the entrance to the uterus. The cervix responds to the pelvic, hypo-gastric, and vagus nerve-systems, while the clitoris uses mostly the pudendal nerve-system. (This is to say, cervical orgasms feel entirely different for your partner than clitoral.)

Cervical orgasms are produced through repetitive deep penetrations either by your fingers or your penis (this is where those advanced PC muscle exercises really come in handy - see the next chapter) as you push deeply into the cervix inside of your partner's vaginal canal. If you possess the sexual stamina necessary to induce a penetrative, cervical orgasm, both you and your partner will know when she has experienced this. If she has already had a clitoral or G-Spot orgasm prior to the build up of her cervical orgasm, it will be easier to achieve (often taking somewhere between four to fifteen minutes of penetration).

Women have described a deep sense of release when experiencing a cervical orgasm (similar to feelings that can be induced by the G-spot orgasm). Some have experienced emotional breakthroughs that allowed them to release old trauma or emotional pain. They felt open, free, and loving as if for the first time after they first experienced a cervical orgasm with a partner.

Imagine having tension in your lower back for your entire life and not knowing that it was a kind of tension that could be released. The first time you met a masseuse who could relieve you of your lower back tension in the course of one session would be transformational and life-changing. I assume you would be quite grateful to that masseuse. In my research for this book, I have had several women describe their first cervical orgasm in much the same way. Their entire bodies started to tingle, they had repetitive vaginal contractions, and, after they climaxed, they felt deeply relaxed as is for the first time in their entire lives. The deep sense of release and closeness that they felt upon achieving a cervical orgasm (including a rush of oxytocin- the connection hormone) brought them and their partners closer together than anything else they had ever experienced.

Raise your sexual stamina, connect emotionally with your woman and make sure that she feels relaxed, and make your way up through this three part hierarchy of orgasmic bliss.

## Dedicated Sex Dates

The best way to most fully connect with your partner on a regular basis is by planning dedicated sex dates.

Many people believe that sex has to have spontaneity to be really hot, or charged. But do you enjoy going to a sporting event, getting a massage, or exercising any less just because it was in your calendar? Of course not. And similar to physical exercise, if you don't get these dates locked into your schedule, sex might not occur as frequently as you'd like. Literally bring out your calendar and schedule dedicated sex dates with your partner.

Explain to her that you want to actively work on your relationship. Tell her you want to be the kind of couple that is so connected that other people admire them. Ask her how she would feel if you had a weekly sex date where your mutual sole intention was to explore each other's bodies more fully. And as long as you are presenting this in a giving context such as "I want to understand your body and make you feel as amazing as possible," how can she possibly not say yes to that?

Agree with your partner on one or two nights a week that are non-negotiable sex date nights. When the night arrives, turn your phones off, remove all distractions, hire a babysitter- whatever you need to do to make it happen.

Take the time to explore, savor, and enjoy each other's bodies again. See who can make the other orgasm the most intensely. Learn each other's sexual likes and dislikes to the point of having them memorized. You should know your partner's body better than you know the back of your own hand.

Maybe sinking your teeth into her neck during sex sets her over the edge that much faster. Maybe she feels safer when your torsos are touching or perhaps she wants frequent verbal reassurance that you love her. Maybe she wants as much of your weight on her as possible so she feels more secure under your pressure. You'll never know all of her likes and dislikes until you set aside the time to really explore.

Become experts on each other's sexual arousal and your relationship will prosper.

# Being a Sexual Beast

By being your best, your relationship can be its best. There are many ways that you can level up your bedroom skills and beliefs about your sexual abilities.

Sexual performances rise and fall so if you've ever felt sexually inadequate, you are far from alone. Everyone has bouts of performance anxiety, sexual dysfunction, or other sex-related stressors.

We will work on improving your mental game, enhancing your sexual strength, and managing your sexual energy. The idea is to get you to be your best possible sexual self so that you can consistently show your partner a mind-blowing performance.

## Stop Watching Porn

Many studies have shown that porn consumption is hazardous to your psychological and sexual health. It damages the intimacy in your relationship, affects the strength of your erections, and weakens your attraction to your partner.

Just as fast food is a false form of nutrition, pornography is a false form of intimacy.

In one session of porn consumption, you're able to view hundreds of sexually available, airbrushed women playing out your every sexual fantasy. So when it comes time to being with your partner in bed, your routinely overstimulated brain experiences difficulty reaching arousal.

Porn addiction is what is known as an "arousal addiction." Instead of wanting more of the same of something (like drug addiction), you crave more varied stimulation. You are ultimately trapping yourself in an endless spiral of insatiability. Your brain cannot allow you to experience sexual satisfaction with your partner simply because it doesn't offer enough variety. Bottom line, porn is poisoning your sex life.

## Benefits of Eliminating Porn Consumption

While your porn use is probably far from being a classifiable issue, even mild consumption negatively affects your sex drive, your perception of your partner, and your overall relationship .

The benefits of reducing and removing porn from your life include

- More control over your orgasm
- Increased sex drive
- Stronger and longer lasting erections
- Increased sexual attraction to your partner
- More mental and emotional presence with your partner
- More appreciation of women in general

Here are three tips on how to cut back and eventually eliminate your porn consumption.

## 1. Commit to only viewing one actress' work

Limiting your consumption to viewing the work of only one actress is the lesser of two evils when compared to overconsumption. Instead of randomly clicking through hundreds of different porn stars, you are conditioning your brain to respond to one individual actress. By limiting your consumption in this way, you reduce the likelihood of being overstimulated by mass variety.

## 2. Cut down time spent watching porn

Reduce your normal porn consumption. Cut down to viewing porn only once or twice a week. Set a timer for ten to twenty minutes to avoid binging during your sessions. Schedule it, if you need to, but set a hard boundary. Make it non-negotiable and stick to it.

## 3. Try the 90-day experiment

What I have found to be the most effective way to eliminate porn use is the 90 Day Experiment. Go cold turkey and do not watch porn for 90 days. Get a friend to hold you accountable if necessary.

# The Exception

There is one exception that I recommend to my clients regarding porn use. If you find that you really want some visual stimulation to get your mind going when masturbating, make and use porn of your partner.

Bring it up honestly. Tell your partner that you read that porn was bad for your sexual health, and, while you aren't a heavy user by any means, you would like to cut it from your life entirely. Explain that you would love if it you had material of her to masturbate to whenever you are apart (e.g., when one of you is travelling, etc.). Letting your partner know that you are choosing to masturbate solely to material of her is a way to express how desirable you find her.

You get better at whatever you are doing in any moment. So by training your brain to masturbate to your partner, you continually increase your sexual attraction to her.

## Sexually Strengthening Exercises

According to ancient Taoist sexual philosophy, feminine energy is like water and masculine energy is like fire. Men can either use the water to quickly douse the fire (premature ejaculation) or the fire can learn to burn brightly for long enough that it brings the water to a boil.

So how do you keep your fire burning brightly? What can you do to satisfy your partner more deeply?

Here are the 7 sexually strengthening exercises that I give to my clients. These will ensure that you will be able to keep your partner feeling sexually fulfilled.

## 1. Exercise Regularly

Exercise can raise your testosterone levels and give you endorphin and dopamine rushes.

As men age, they naturally produce less testosterone over time. Exercise has been proven to stabilize testosterone levels and keep men's libido thriving later into their lives.

The more muscle groups that you put stress on, the more testosterone your body produces to heal your muscles. Find an active hobby outside of the gym that engages multiple muscle groups (like dance class, rock climbing, yoga, boxing, etc.). And in the gym? Keep it simple with compound exercises like squats, pull-ups, push-ups, and burpees.

Another factor to consider is that exercise reduces stress levels and stress is huge a libido killer. If you have a lot going on in your life (and who doesn't?) that causes you chronic stress, exercise is one of the most effective stress busters available.

## 2. Improve Your Diet

Even in small amounts, sugar, caffeine, nicotine, and alcohol all negatively affect your libido and erectile strength. They do so because they are all either stimulants or depressants and they alter your body's natural chemical make up. If any of these drugs are particularly present in your life (I'm looking at you, coffee drinkers) then you might want to cut back a bit.

## 3. Sleep Well

Testosterone (the sex and aggression hormone) is produced during the night. If your sleep has been lacking then you likely have low testosterone levels.

Remember, testosterone is responsible for regulating your sex drive, so you want to keep this one coming. Also, by lacking in sleep you produce more of the stress-hormone cortisol… which is a double hit against your sex drive (if you aren't producing enough testosterone and you are producing cortisol- both of which hinder your arousal).

There are a couple quick and easy things you can do to improve your sleep quality:

- Don't eat anything within two hours of bedtime
- Turn off all artificial light sources (television, computer, cell phone, blinking lights, etc.) at least an hour before bed
- Develop a sleep routine. People are creatures of habit; we sleep better when we consistently go to bed at the same time

## 4. Practice Yoga

The vast majority of men have overly tight hips, hamstrings, and lower backs. These parts of your body are used heavily during sex and if they are stronger and more flexible, you will have less muscular tension throughout your body (the less tense you are, the greater control you have over your climax) and you will be less sore after a lengthy sex session.

## 5. Tongue And Jaw Strengthening Exercise

Ever had your tongue or jaw cramp up during oral sex? It definitely isn't fun for you or (especially) for her.

Strengthen your jaw and tongue muscles by doing tongue push-ups. Push the underside of the tip of your tongue into the front of your hard palate (the front of the roof of your mouth, right behind your front teeth). Do this enough times with enough strength and it will become easier over time (giving you more sexual stamina for oral sex).

To take this exercise to the next level you can start putting hard-shelled chocolate candies between your tongue and the hard palate and practice crushing them with your tongue's force (or use grapes for a healthier alternative).

## 6. Pelvic Floor Muscle Exercises

Ever heard of the PC muscle? The pubococcygeus (PC) muscle is a hammock-shaped muscle that stretches from your pubic bone to your tailbone. It forms your pelvic floor and exists in both men and women. It is the muscle that you can engage when you are peeing to stop the flow of urine.

In many people, these muscles are largely ignored and they begin to weaken over time. Having a strong pelvic floor increases erectile strength, ejaculatory control, and the strength of your orgasms.

To get a greater awareness of your PC muscle, occasionally pulse and hold the muscle to give it a wake up call. Similar to the tongue strengthening exercise, you will feel it becoming easier over time. Start with quick pulses, move up to sets of ten two-second holds, and then after a few days see if you can do ten five-seconds holds without much of a break in between.

## 7. Next Level Pelvic Floor Exercises

The preceding exercises are great to get a relationship with your PC muscle, but you don't build a muscle by going to the gym and flexing your arm for half an hour (not much of a muscle at least).

Muscles need to be challenged to grow. So how can you challenge your PC muscle to grow into a sub-waistline six-pack?

Masturbate to arousal and drape a dry hand towel over your erection. With the towel in place, do penis push-ups by flexing your PC muscle and lifting the towel.

To increase the difficulty of this exercise, use a wet hand towel once you have mastered the dry hand towel push up. After that, you can upgrade to a small dry beach towel. These exercises are not for the faint of heart, but I promise, even doing five minutes a day a few times per week will make a noticeable difference in erectile strength and ejaculatory control. Try it out and see what results you experience.

## Managing Your Sexual Energy

Evidence (known for centuries by the ancient Taoists) suggests that ejaculating less often could make you into a more productive, driven, and loving man.

Your sexual energy is the greatest and most potent form of energy available to you. You can either squander it or utilize it to its fullest potential and let it supercharge your life.

## How It Works

As many men know, sexual energy can be a powerful, all-encompassing beast.

Semen retention is something that high-level professional athletes have practiced for a long time. Do you think Tyson would have bit Holyfield's ear off if he had masturbated right before the fight? I highly doubt it.

The number one biologically hard-wired task that all mammals seek is reproduction. If your body thinks that you are already doing well in terms of reproduction (because you are ejaculating often), then it doesn't stay motivated to conquer life, or accumulate resources, or acquire a mate, etc.

By refraining from frequent orgasms, your testosterone (or aggression) levels experience a boost and you're more likely to dominate whatever task you're tackling.

There is a drop in testosterone levels immediately following an ejaculation which makes your mojo drop. Testosterone is present in both men and women and is largely responsible for sexual desire and aggression.

You've likely felt the unique sense of numbness that permeates your mind after climax. Now imagine that numbness encompassing your daily mental state as a result of indulging in ejaculation too frequently.

## What Are The Benefits?

You will experience a handful of positive side effects when you refrain from frequent ejaculation.

**There are the benefits that have been proven scientifically:**

- More energy
- Better concentration
- Deeper voices
- Interacting with sexual mates more easily
- Greater gains from workouts
- Stronger erections
- Return to healthier sexual tastes (i.e. easier to do with away with porn)
- More optimism

**There are also the benefits that I have seen with my clients and that I have personally experienced:**

- Greater focus

- Massively increased productivity
- Greater appreciation for "real" women (irather than the airbrushed women found in porn)
- More sexually polarized intercourse with partners
- Greater depth within intimate relationships
- Deeper connection with and love for partners

# How To Harness Your Sexual Energy

Your best results will come when you continue to engage in sexual activity while refraining from orgasm because the more sexual energy you have in your reserves, the more you have to utilize to fully open your partner.

You want to be revving up your internal engine without blowing a gasket.

Here is the process that my clients have consistently found to be the easiest way to transition into harnessing their sexual energy.

## 1. Commit to trying it

You do not have continue to refrain from frequent ejaculation if you decide it isn't for you. Just *try* it. Give it a week and see what happens. Understand that while most men experience positive results when they learn to harness their sexual energy, this process does not have to be one you commit to doing for the rest of your life.

## 2. Take the first 2-3 days off completely

Don't masturbate; don't have sex. Remove all of the stressors that you can from your life. Sleep well, and generally take good care of yourself. This will help you get you away from masturbating simply because you think you *should*. It will help you transition back to becoming aware of your body (in fashion similar to eating food because "it's noon and therefore, lunchtime" as opposed to eating when you experience hunger). A lot of this process is about re-sensitizing your mind to your sexual self.

## 3. Between the 3-7 day mark, begin exploring sexual pleasure again

...but keep a safe distance from the orgasmic 'point of no return'. If you think of your sexual arousal on a scale of 1 to 10, practice intentionally rising and falling your arousal between the 4-8 range while engaging sexually with (or without) your partner. Doing this will not only stoke your sexual fires, but it will get you more comfortable with determining your ejaculatory 'point of no return'; knowing this will allow you more control over your orgasm. It will also prevent you from experiencing premature ejaculation with your partner.

Additionally, the more sexual energy you have to utilize in your sex life, the more you will want to make your partner achieve orgasm. The more you make her achieve orgasm, the more testosterone spikes you experience. It's truly a win-win situation.

## 4. Recognize your response to the increased sexual energy

You might notice feeling more driven and decisive, more rested on less sleep. and as though you're standing taller- like your posture has improved. You may be more present and aware in your social interactions. It's possible you'll feel simultaneously more emotionally connected to your partner and more grounded in your masculinity. You may feel more proficient at dialing up and down your polarity, with communication AND sex flowing easily.

If you experience feelings of anxiety or agitation, or if you get a really overwhelming urge to come, channel that energy into something productive. Go to the gym, go for a run, meditate, or do something creative. Redirect the energy into something that benefits you.

It's that simple. Have fewer orgasms, gain mental clarity, and be able to open your partner more fully.

# What To Do Now

By this point you have read many paradigm-shifting concepts that have changed how you look at your partner and your relationship.

The most important thing that you can do at this point is to make sure that you are consistently taking action.

You could read a thousand books on how to become a better surfer, but if you haven't physically practiced standing on a surfboard for any length of time, then you won't become any better.

Education is one half of the picture; experience is the other.

So if you haven't been implementing the concepts throughout the book while you learn them, I implore you to take that first step.

Think of your favorite tip. Maybe it was a specific Power Compliment in the first section of the book. Maybe Improving Communication reminded you that there is something in your relationship (or in your life) that you need to apologize for. Maybe the section on Supercharging

Your Sex Life reminded you to go to the gym or make your sex life a focused priority again.

Whatever it is, take action.

You know what to do; now it's just a matter of doing it.

I believe in you!

# Closing Comments

Congratulations for making it to the end of this book. I read once that over 90% of people don't make it to the end of the books they read, so the fact that you made it here really says something about your commitment to yourself and your relationship (GO YOU!).

As you read this book, I hope that you picked up on some recurring themes throughout the different sections.

1. Women respond well to being actively loved.
2. It is less about what you say or do for your partner and more about *why* you said or did those things. The reason behind your actions is what makes her feel loved and cared for.
3. By putting your efforts towards a few small but key areas, you can see a huge amount of positive change in your relationship very quickly.

And before we wrap up here, I want to talk to you about patience.

As men, we are all too often racing towards an imaginary finish line. We have all of our goals and tasks up in our heads and we want to plow through them as quickly as possible so that *someday* we can let ourselves be happy. But it's important to balance your striving nature with contentment.

Be patient with your growth, your life, her moods, and your relationship… all things take time.

Do you ever see the couple in public that makes everyone's heads turn with how in love they appear to be? They didn't just fall into that kind of a relationship with zero effort. The relationships that thrive are the ones that contain two self-aware, loving, and grateful partners who strive to make each other's lives that much easier.

In closing, if you make her feel seen, appreciated, and loved, the rest will fall into place. Building your relationship into something amazing takes effort, but it is so worth it.

Thank you for reading, and if you got a lot out of this book, feel free to recommend it to a close friend who you would like to see be blissfully happy in their relationship.

Dedicated to your success,

Jordan Gray

www.jordangrayconsulting.com

# About the Author

#1 Amazon best-selling author, relationship coach, and jet-setting world traveler, Jordan Gray helps people remove their emotional blocks, and get into (and maintain) thriving intimate relationships.

His thoughts on modern dating and relationships have been featured in numerous print publications, and on radio and television broadcasts internationally.

In his relationship coaching practice, Jordan has worked with thousands of students over the past four years, and has more wedding invitations from his former clients than he can keep up with.

When he's not coaching clients or writing new books, Jordan loves to surf without a wetsuit, immerse himself in new cultures, and savor slow motion hang outs with his closest companions.

You can find his books on Amazon, and you can see more of his writing at www.jordangrayconsulting.com.

Made in the USA
Monee, IL
14 September 2021